This Coloring Book Belongs To:

_____

The Wolf Pack Coloring Book
Volume 3

This book consists of twenty-six wolf images.
They can be colored using crayon, colored pencils,
pastel, or whatever you wish.
Designed to fit in a 8" x 10" standard frame.

Happy Coloring!

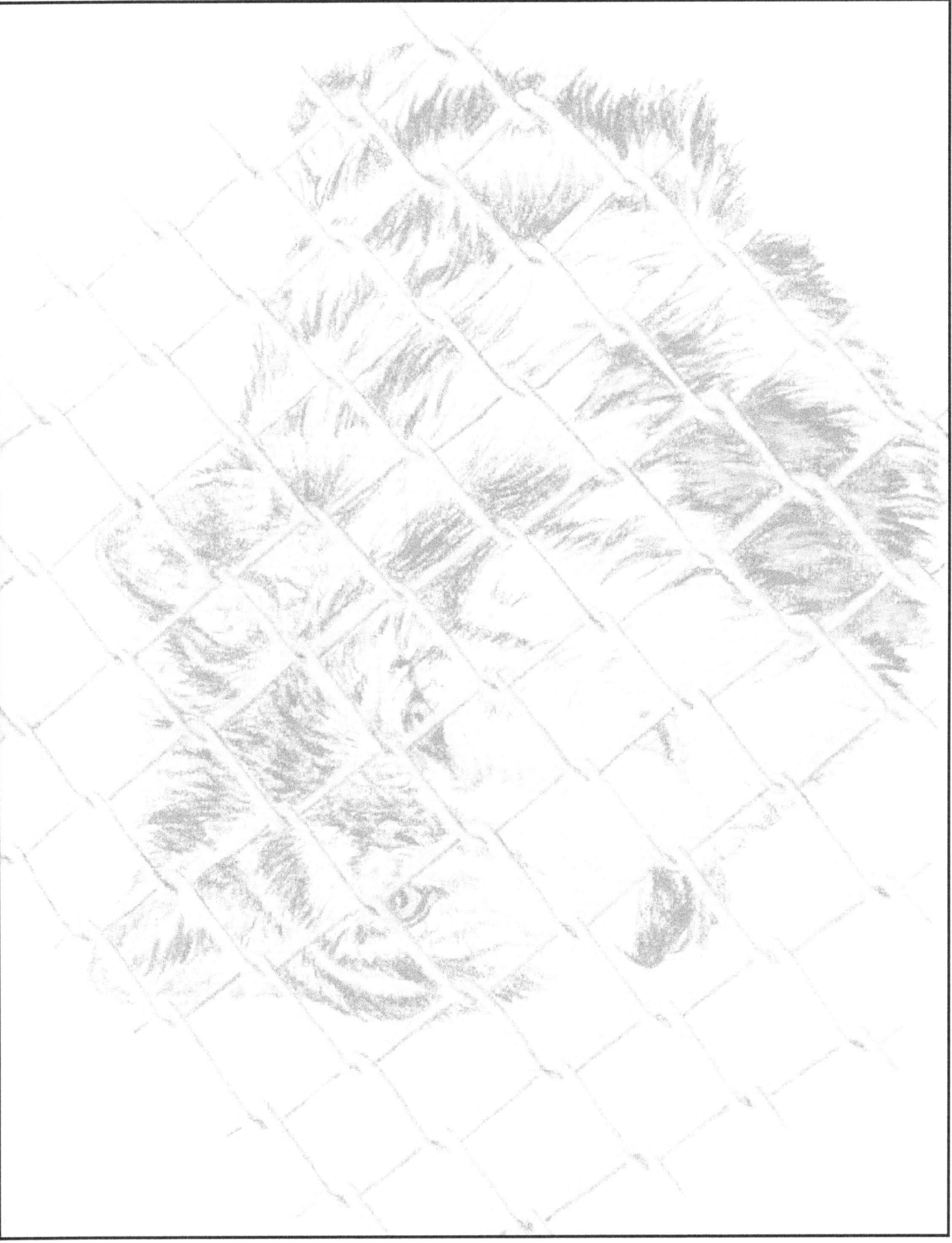

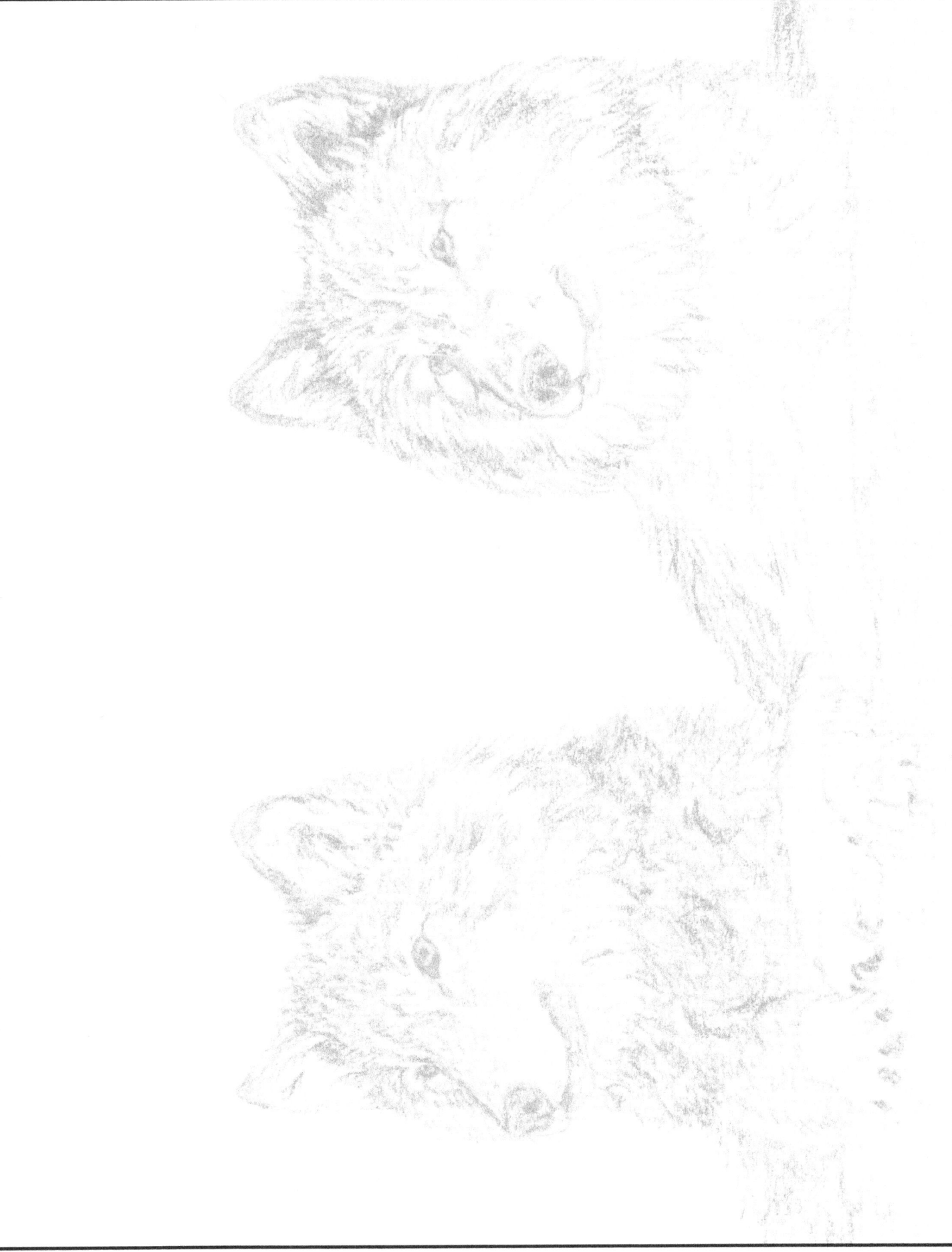

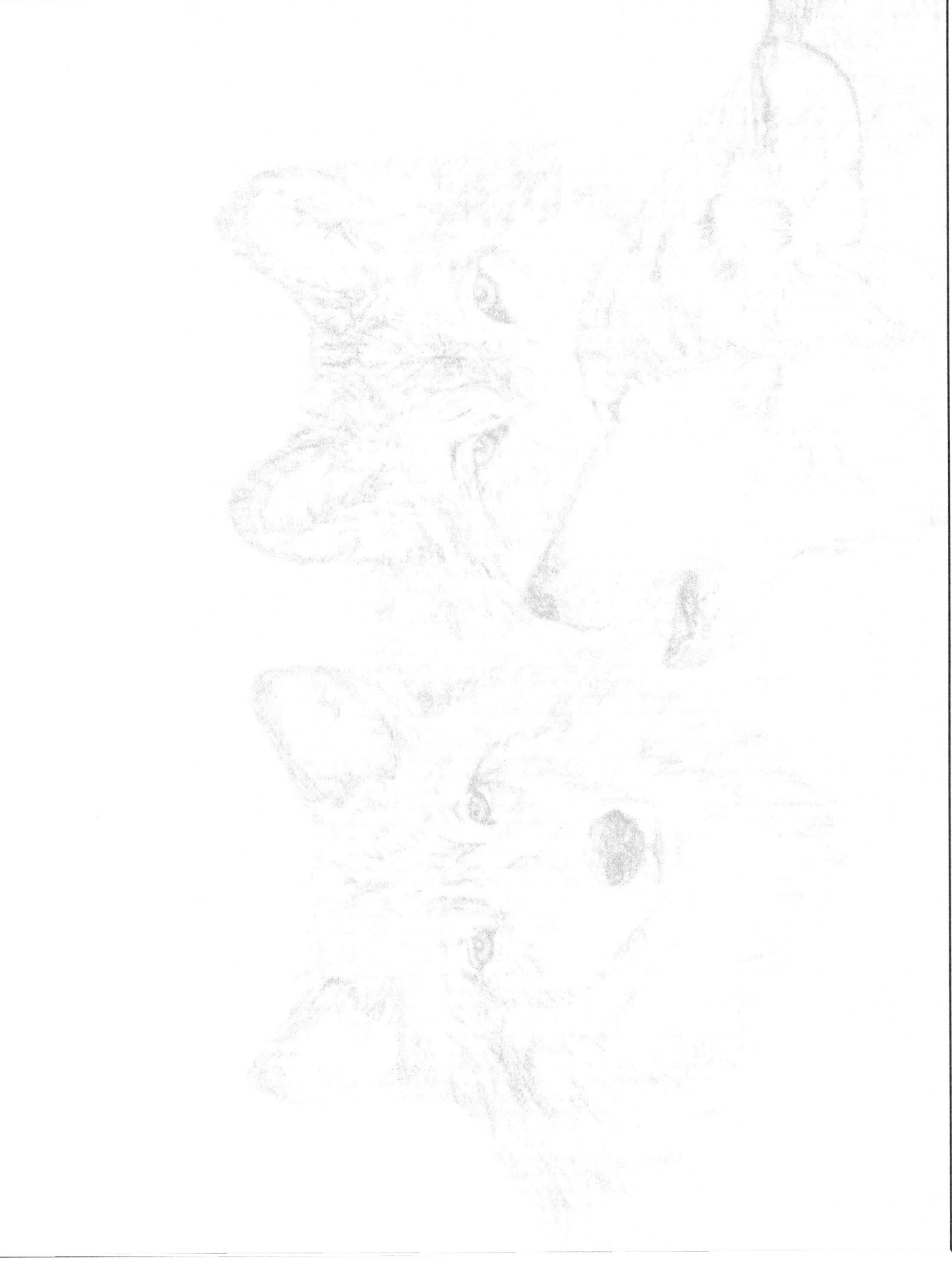

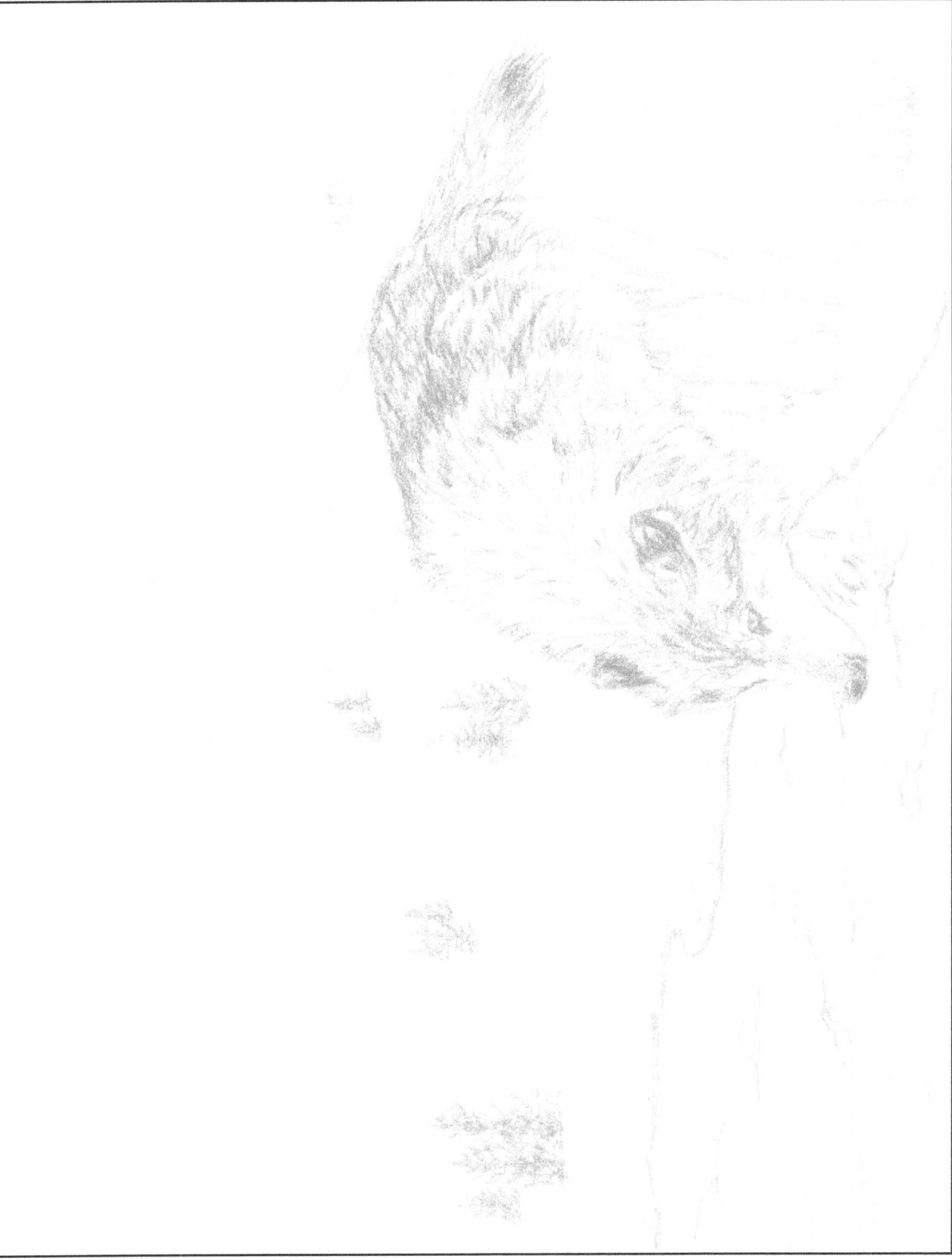

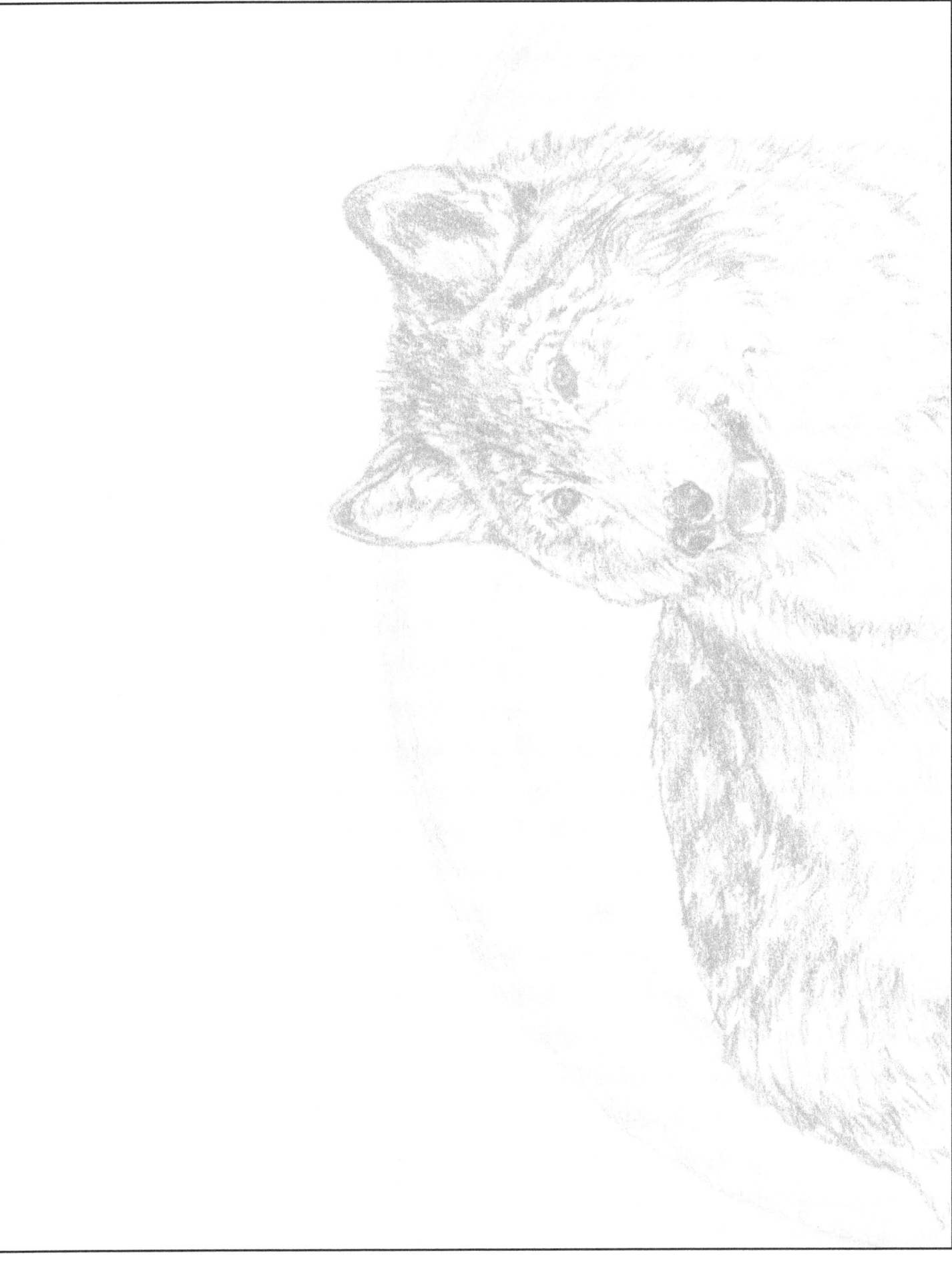

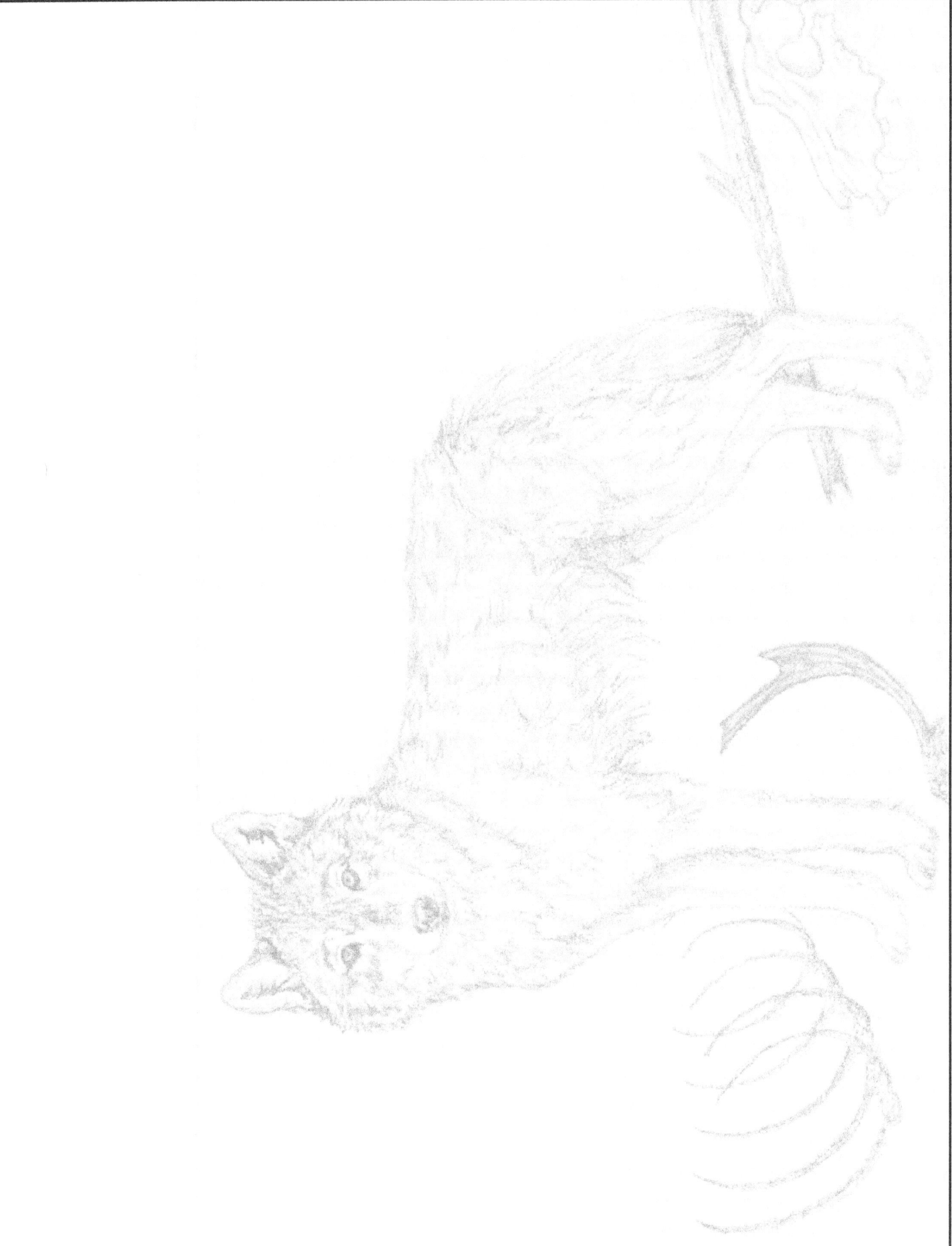

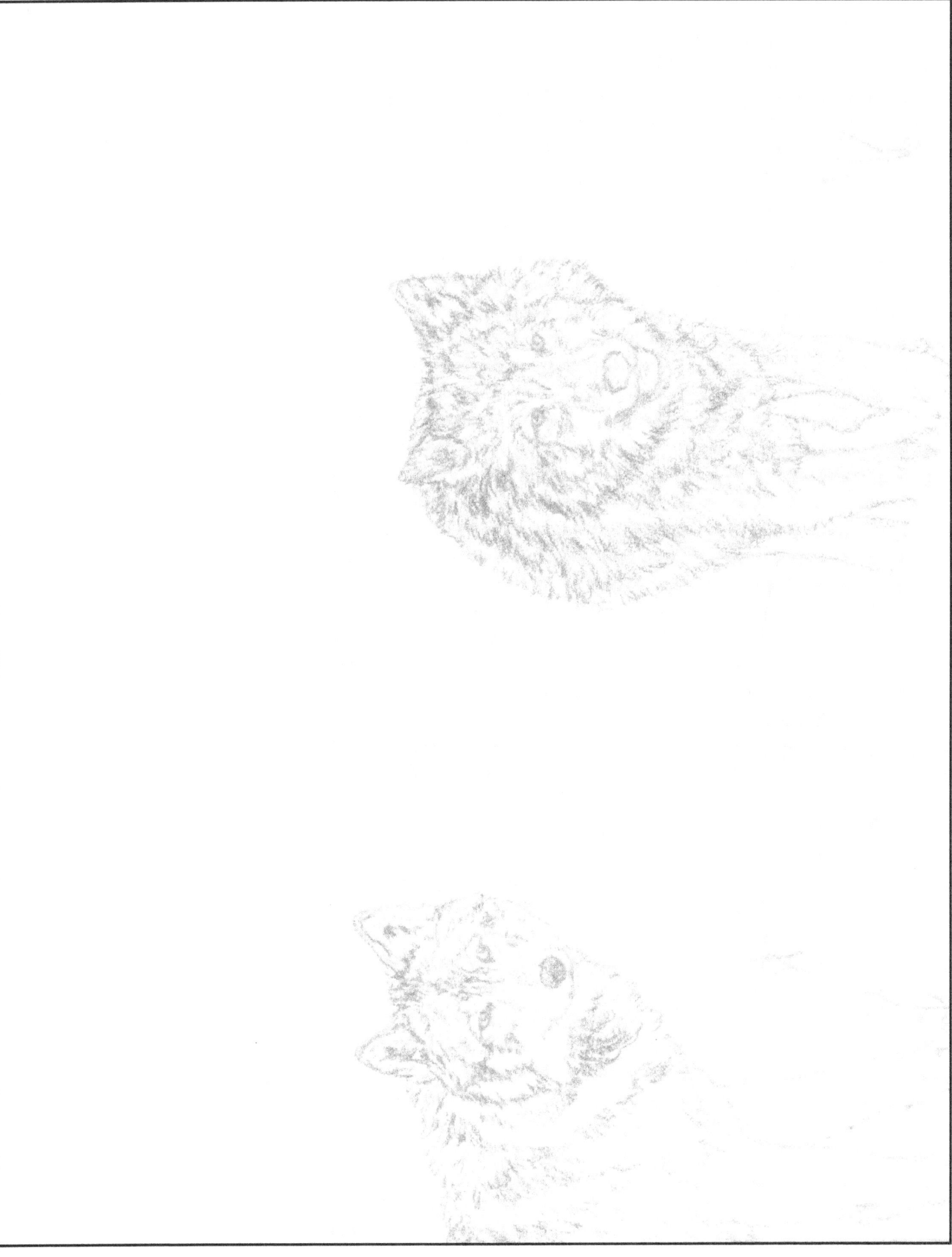

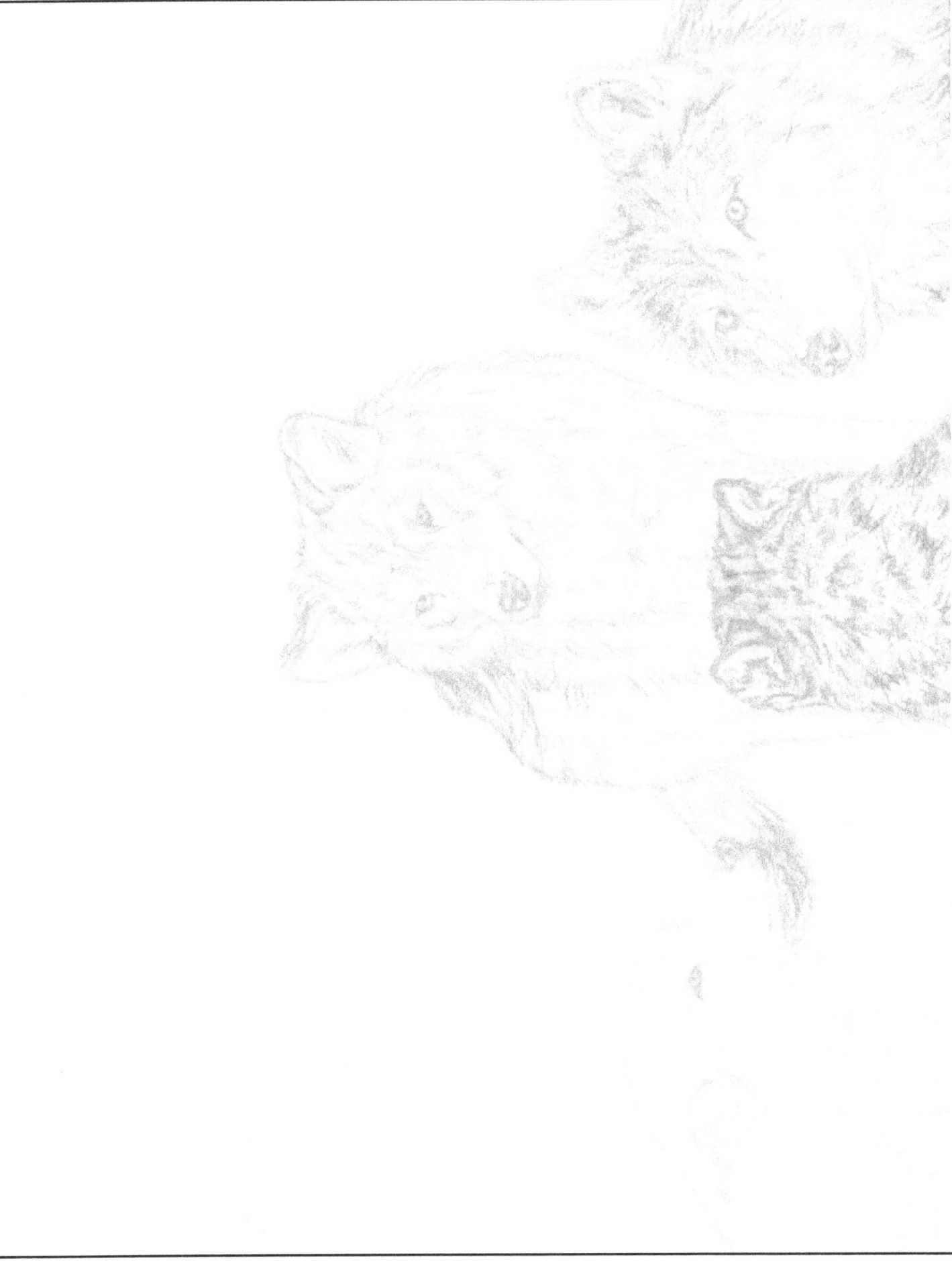

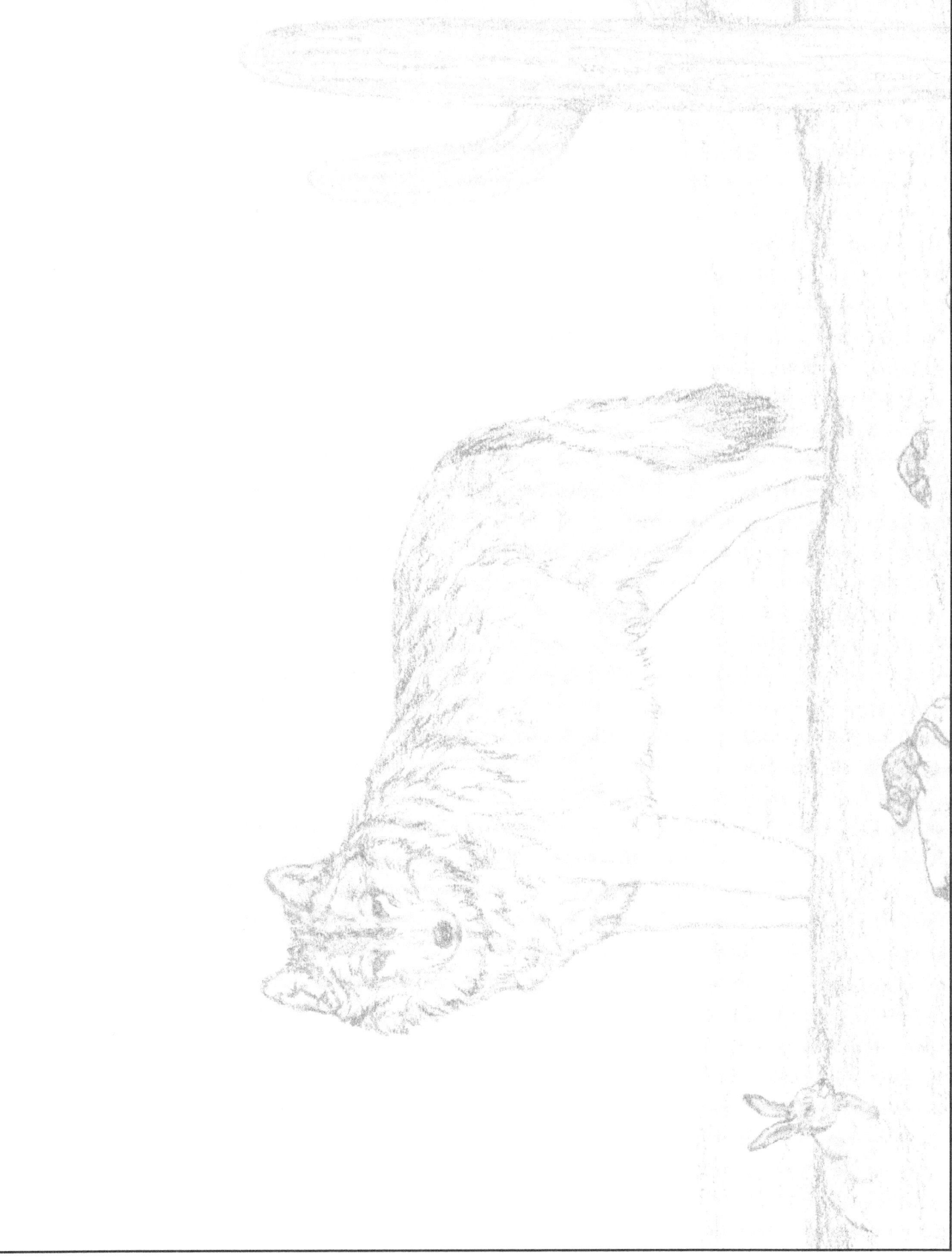

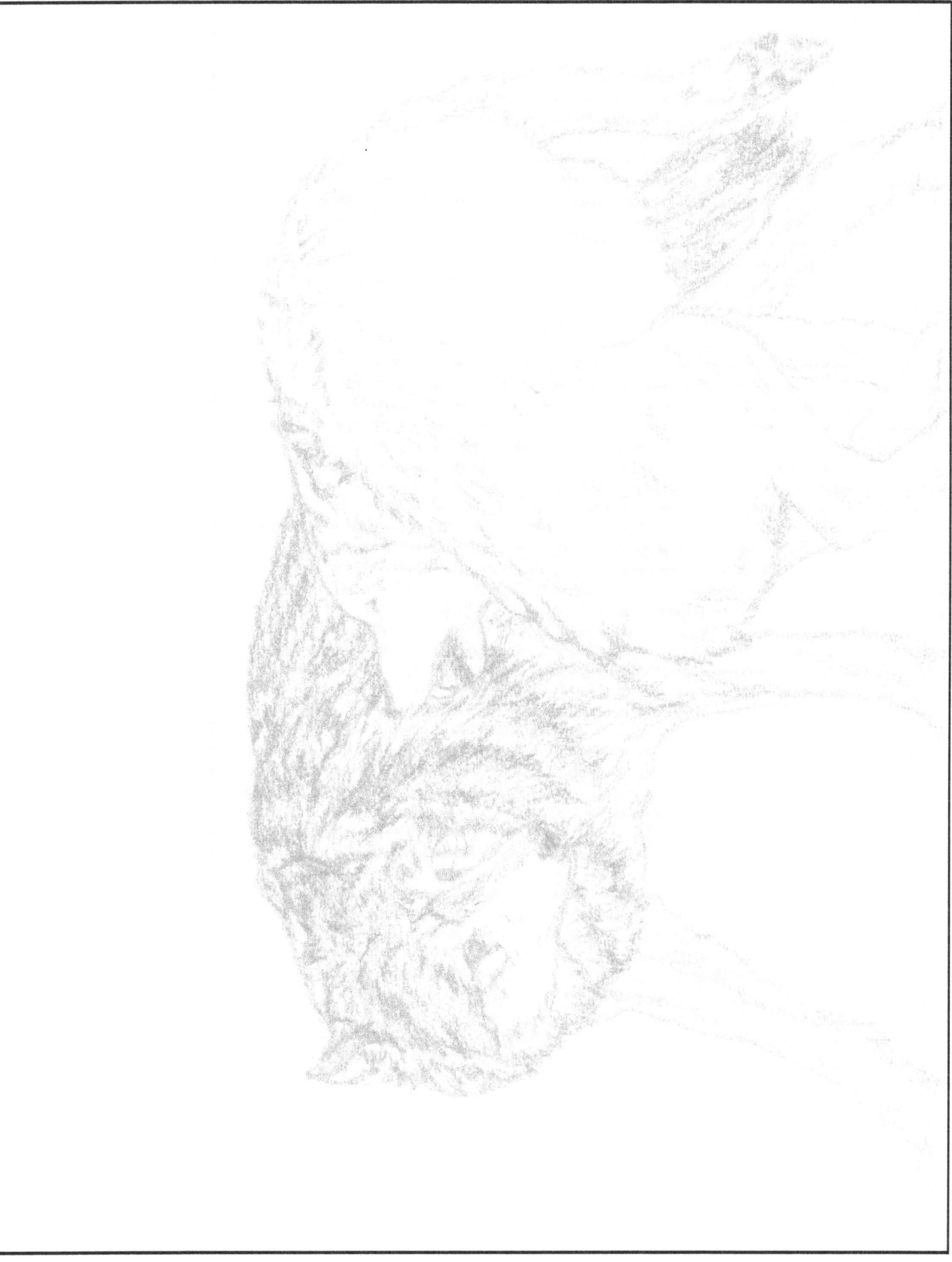

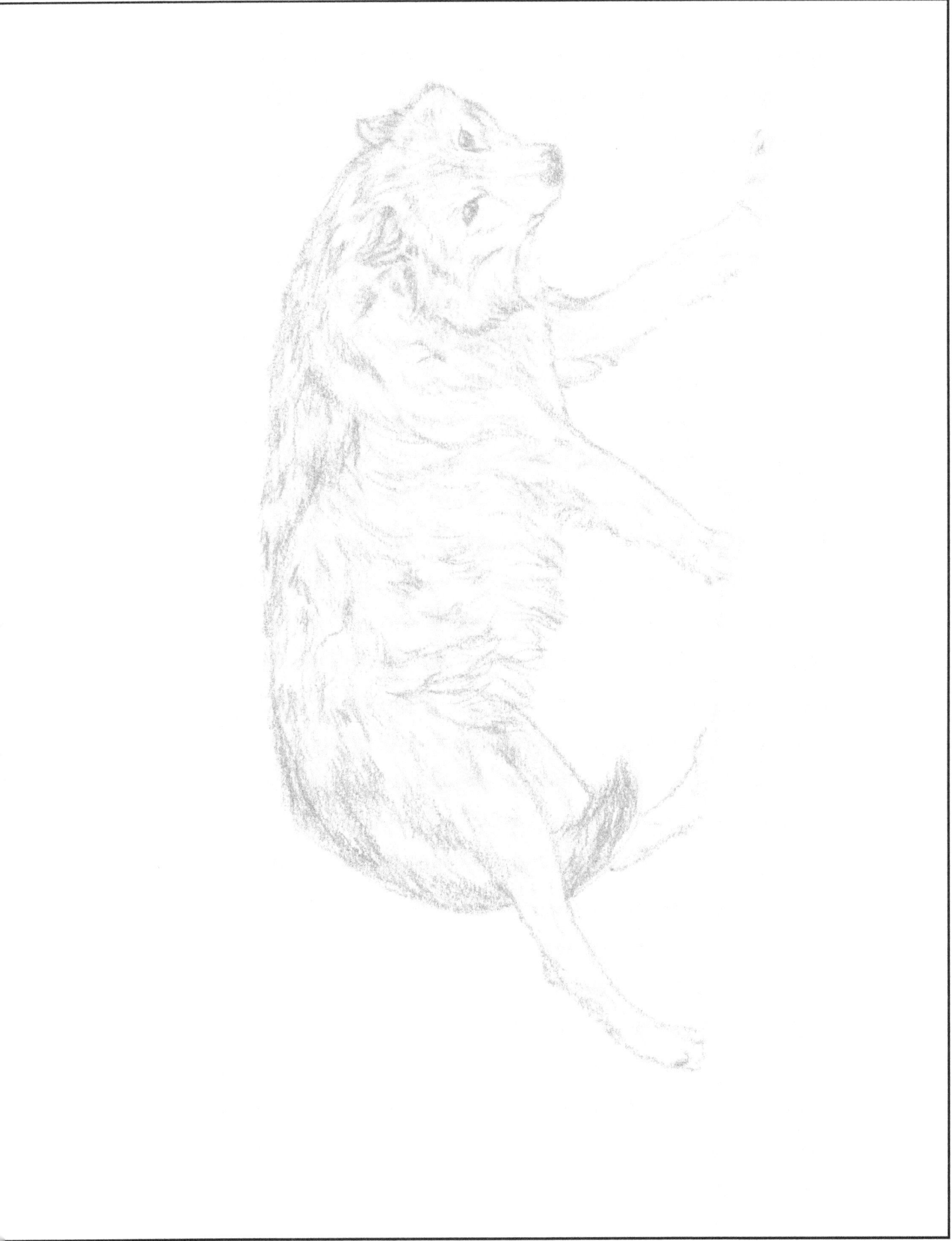

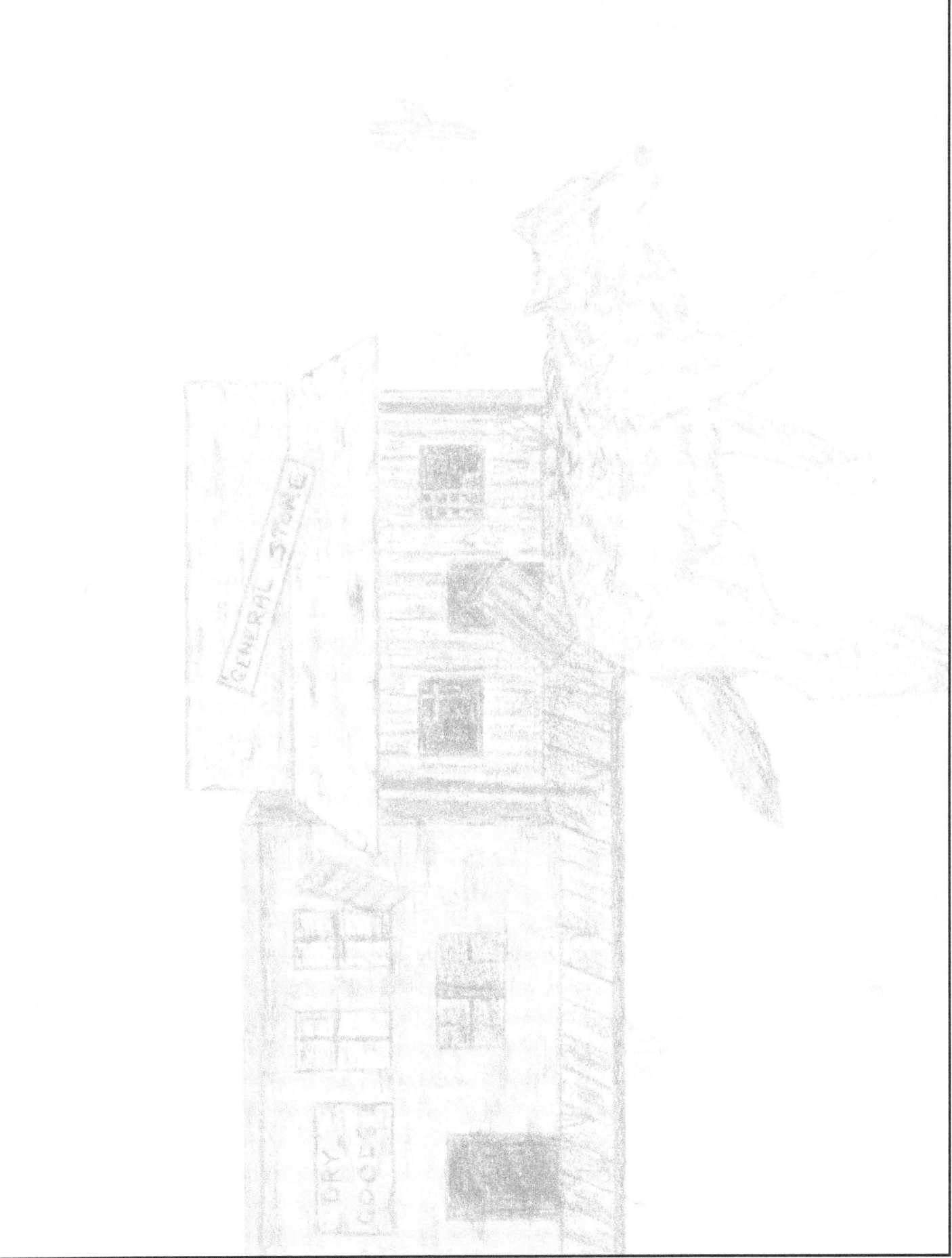

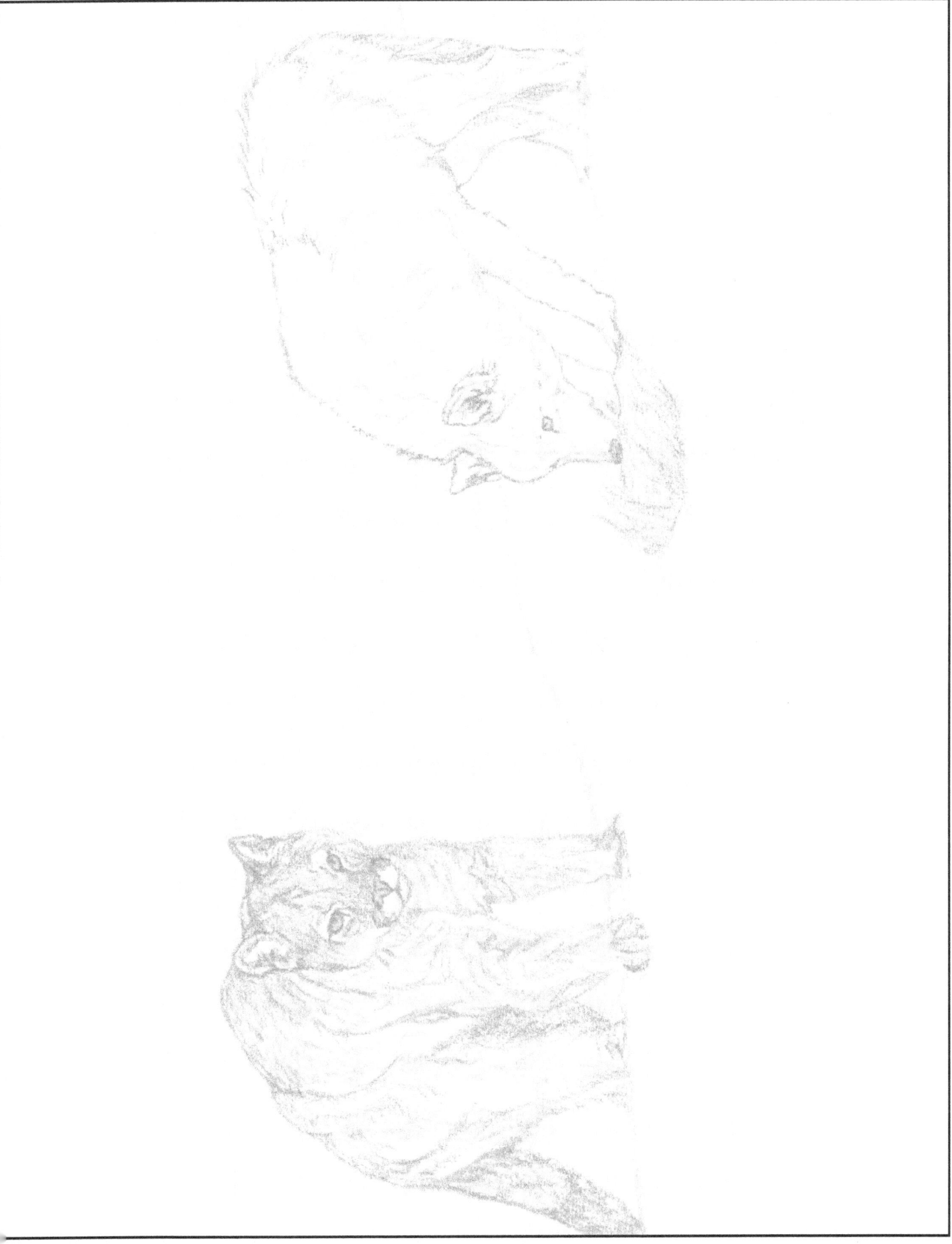

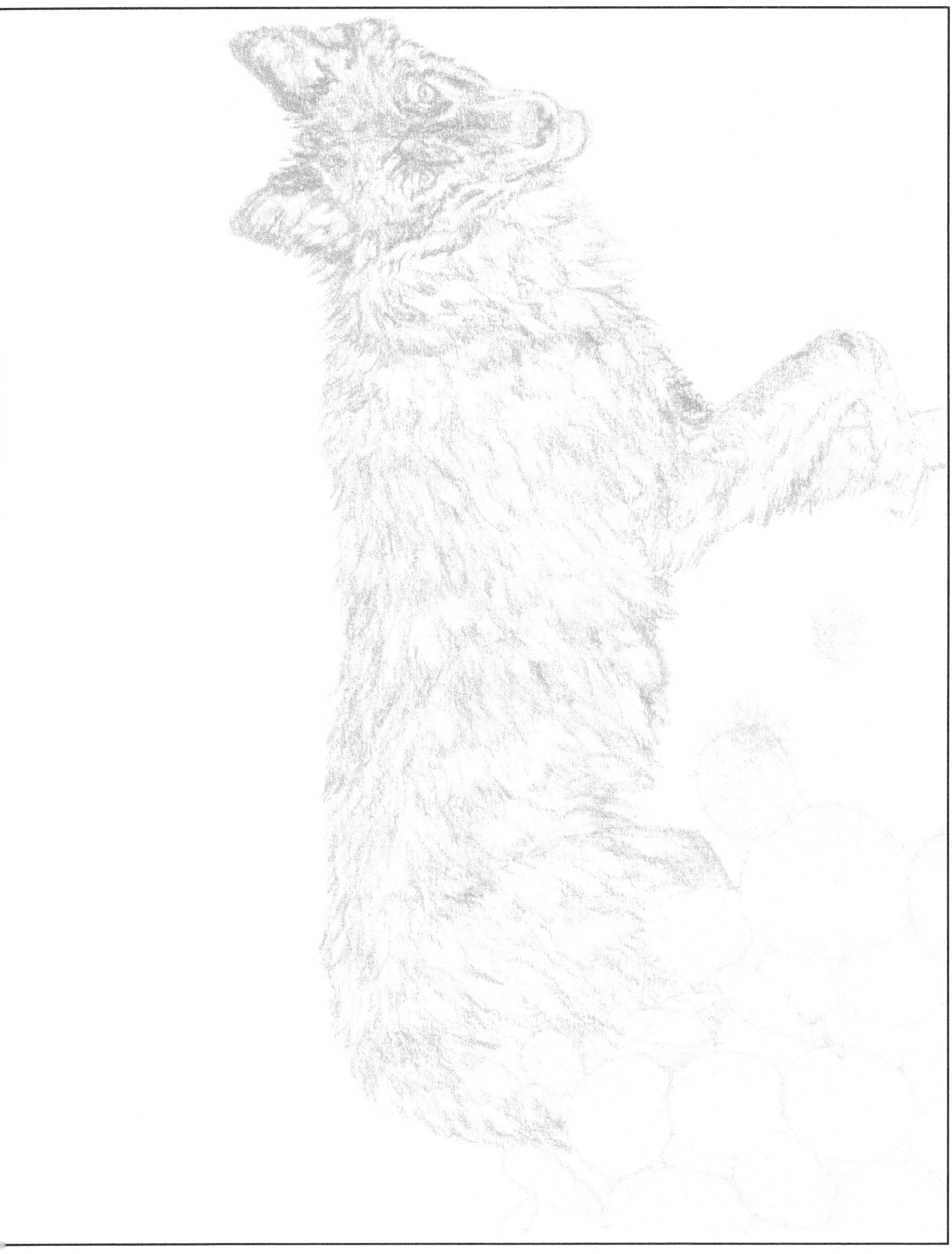

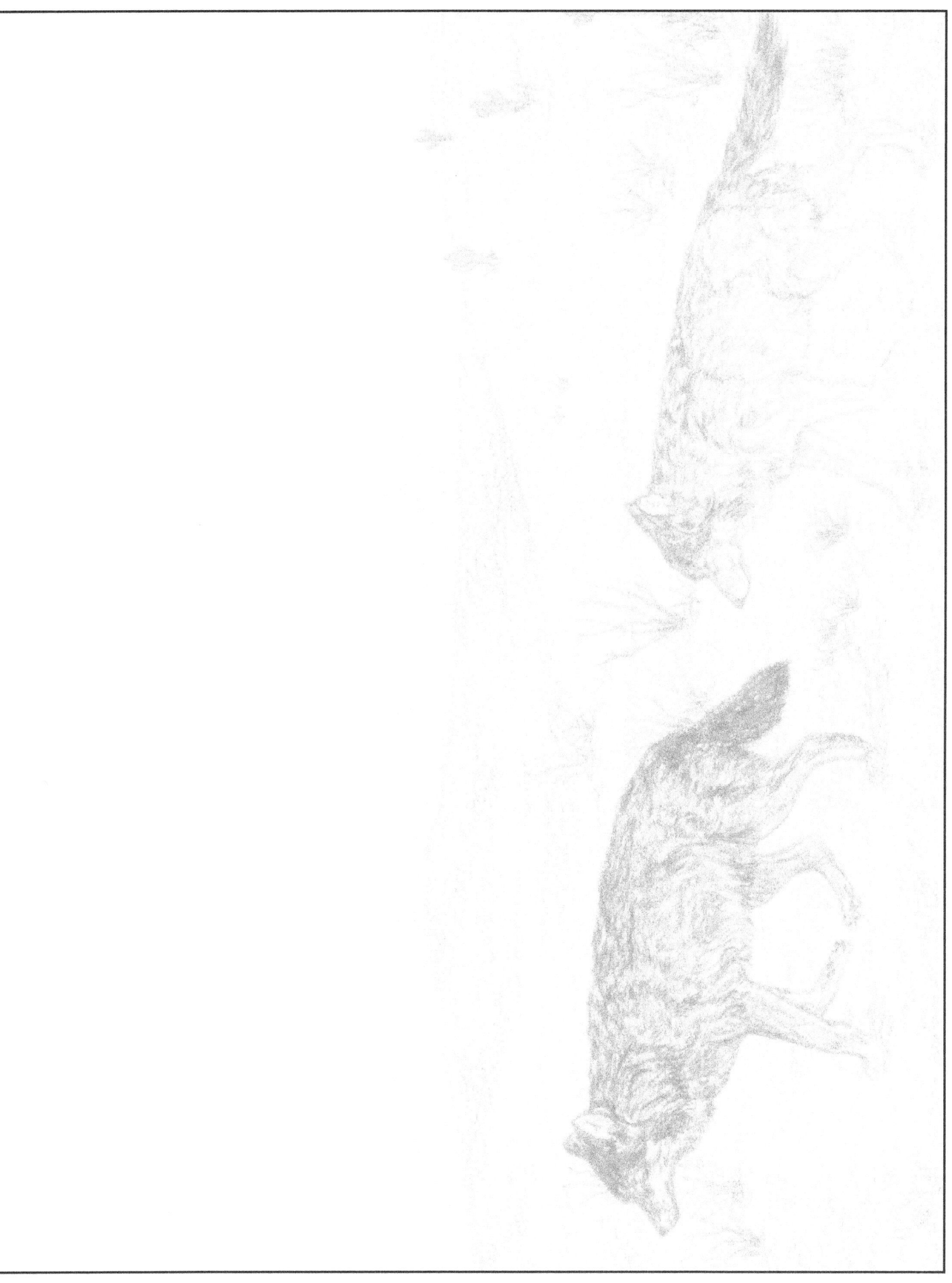